Not My Story To Tell

My journey through grief: Loving and losing a daughter with bi-polar disorder

Cathy Lynn Brooks

ISBN: 1976029503
ISBN 13: 9781976029509

For my husband Greg who lived this life with me.

THE WILD WEST

"My mother...was perfectly horrified when I began shooting and tried to keep me in school, but I would run away and go quail shooting in the woods or trim my dresses with wreaths of wildflowers."

Annie Oakley

My daughter lived large. She did things her way and when she did something she did it in a huge way. There was nothing mediocre in the way she lived her life. She had strong convictions and she stuck by them. She always learned lessons the hard way. She was an individual and she didn't care what others thought of her.

Justine cared deeply about the homeless, abused women and the mentally ill. She did one high school co-op placement in a drop in centre for people who live on the street and another in a shelter for abused women. She completed her forty hours of community service in a soup kitchen where she served food and conversed with the people who ate dinner there. She didn't just talk about problems she took action.

She loved her family and friends and was very loyal. She lived by her own standards. As I write about her, I'm often reminded of a woman from the Wild West. Annie Oakley or some woman dressed in cowboy clothes with guns comes to mind. She was a person who would not take crap from anyone but had a heart of gold.

INTRODUCTION

I was working in an inner city elementary school directly across the street from a women's shelter. We had many students who had behavioural problems and other serious issues. The program support department teacher and I started a self-esteem program with some female grade seven and eight leaders of the school and some troubled girls. We had no idea we would uncover some very deep secrets of abuse.

I was running this program when Justine was six years old and told me she didn't want me to leave her with her male babysitter. I was immediately on high alert. I had known other people who had been sexually abused as children and I was not naive about this topic. This was not going to happen to my child. I had already told her to be discreet when using the bathroom and to close the door. I told her to make sure she changed in private. Boys would be embarrassed to see that.

Justine went to a nursery school run by a former colleague and very good friend of mine. Meribeth had made all her little pupils aware of not allowing anyone to touch their private parts and most especially to tell a trusted adult if this ever happened. Justine was well trained and we were very open to discussing any topic at in our home. I was raised in the sixties and seventies and my generation was comfortable discussing sex and our bodies. There were no secrets in our home.

In a very calm and welcoming voice, I asked her why she didn't want Sam to babysit. She said she just didn't. I asked in a different way. She answered slightly sassy. I told her that she didn't get to choose her babysitters. I was satisfied with her answers and knew she would tell me if anyone tried to hurt her.

PROLOGUE

The entire time I was writing this book, I had a nagging feeling that I was betraying Justine in some way. She was always very open about her life and she wanted to help others so I know she wouldn't mind me remembering her life and wanting to preserve it. A counsellor once told me it is not my story to tell. That has stayed with me for decades. I've never told much of this to anyone because of what that counsellor said.

Many parts of this book will be surprising and shocking. Even those people who knew Justine will find parts of this story revealing. Her life was no secret, but there are episodes that she didn't want to dwell on. Re-telling much of it was heart wrenching, but I don't want one second of it to be lost.

I want those who knew her to know her better and those who never met her to know her. Her life had meaning and I want her never to be forgotten. She lived a lot of life in her twenty-nine years.

That's why I'm telling her story.

AND IT BEGAN...

My daughter will always remain twenty-nine years old. The fact that she got to the age of twenty-nine is nothing short of a miracle. You might wonder if she had a debilitating illness. You might wonder if I was a mother that spent years trying to find a cure for my child. You might wonder why her life seemed so fragile. The answer is all of these things and none of these things. This is the story of Justine's life.

Justine Marie Brooks was born February 5, 1985 in Oshawa, Ontario, Canada. I was thrilled that she was born on her due date and doubly happy that she was born on the fifth of 1985. So neat and easy to remember. I had been so sure I was having a boy that I was surprised but excited she was a girl. I had always pictured having two girls. My parenting philosophy was "two hands two children." She was my first child.

My pregnancy was easy and I thought, healthy. I stopped drinking wine and coffee and I ate too much, but I felt great. I worked fulltime in a residence for young children who had developmental and physical challenges. Lifting heavy children was not required of me since I worked in the behaviour management department but I was young and vibrant, pregnancy was not a disease, so I continued to do so. I also shovelled snow, lifted a heavy mattress when changing the bedding, and did everything I had done before I became pregnant. I was twenty-seven years old and balked when anyone told me to "take it easy." I was not one to take advice and since I felt wonderful, I wanted to continue to do all the things I had done. If I could have given up a baby, I would be a prime candidate to be a surrogate. Pregnancy agreed with me.

My labour and delivery were a different matter. As my labour progressed, my blood pressure increased so high that I had to have a nurse stationed at my bedside and a blood pressure cuff permanently attached to my left arm that filled up with air and cut off my circulation every fifteen minutes. It turns out that the snowflakes I had been seeing were a sign of toxemia and I should have immediately informed my doctor. I should have listened to the people who said to "take it easy." Nonetheless, everything turned out fine and Justine was a healthy, but slightly small baby. She weighed six pounds, thirteen ounces, and she was perfect in every way.

Justine had her very first near-death experience when she was a couple of days old and we were still in the hospital. I was sitting in my bed with my knees up and I had her lying on my knees. My newborn was being soothed by rocking my knees back and forth. Suddenly, I noticed her feet and then quickly her face turning black. I had worked with children for many years and tried not to panic. I thought that maybe she was choking on breast milk. I put her over my shoulder to pat her back and then turned her over. She wasn't breathing! I called for the nurse and I must've blocked the rest out because I can't remember exactly what happened next. Did they get her breathing right away? Did they take her? I know I was so focussed on not panicking and remaining calm that I just waited for them to explain what happened. They said that sometimes the blood rushes to the baby's feet or something like that. I never held a baby like that ever again.

Justine was a perfect baby. She did have colic as a newborn and that caused great stress but after the first three months she was a happy baby, meeting all her milestones and bringing her extended family and us great joy. She was my parents' first grandchild and everyone was delighted with her. She was my husband's family's seventh grandchild but as the story goes, my husband, Greg was his parents' favourite, of their five children. We lived just down the street from my in-laws so it was easy for her be their favourite too.

Considering that Justine was a healthy baby we didn't expect her to be taking her first ambulance ride when she was a few months old. My sister-in-law had looked after her that day. When I went to pick her up, she felt warm and we agreed she might have a fever. I took her home, gave her some Tylenol and put her into a tepid bath. She was burning up with a temperature of 104. I had worked with children all my life and I was very confident I could get her temperature down. As she was laying in the shallow tub, she suddenly went limp while I cradled her in my arms. I was stunned. I had no idea what was going on. I noticed she wasn't breathing. I grabbed her, wrapped her in a towel and tried doing mouth to nose, as I had been trained. I was all alone and I just couldn't believe my baby was lying on the floor not breathing and unconscious.

I called 911. The ambulance seemed to take forever. As they pulled up the driveway I ran out of the house and handed her to one of them. I explained in a panicked voice what had happened. The neighbours came out of their houses and stood watching. The paramedic brought her inside and began looking her over. Within a minute she began breathing. They didn't have any answers for me but we took an ambulance ride to the hospital to have her admitted. She had a fever induced seizure. I have seen hundreds of seizures but had never, and to this day have never, seen one like that.

When Justine was thirteen months old, I got pregnant again and we decided to find a bigger house. Those next few months were a whirlwind. I had taken a part-time job and we were looking for a new home, selling ours, packing up, moving, unpacking and planning for a new baby. Life got very busy. Justine's sister was due on December 19 but decided to wait to be born. As the days got closer and closer to Christmas I began hoping it wouldn't be "today."

Justine was twenty-two months old that Christmas and we knew it was the first Christmas she would understand. I certainly didn't want to be in the hospital and miss it. I always hosted Christmas Eve and that year everyone stayed until well after midnight. I was not concerned because Justine had an afternoon nap every day and I planned to nap with her Christmas afternoon before going to Greg's sister, Gloria's for dinner. Justine was so excited Christmas morning. She woke us up at the crack of dawn. She remained excited all day and could not settle down for a nap. We all went out for a big family dinner at my sister-in-law and brother-in-law's house. Since we were exhausted at nine o'clock we headed home and crawled right into bed. That moment my water broke. It was a long night but Justine got a baby sister, Candice, on December 26, 1986. Again, twenty-six of 1986 just as Justine's birthday was the fifth of 1985. Two months later my sister had my nephew, Eric on February 27 of 1987. Everything seemed to be lining up.

Justine and Candice spent their early childhood living on a circular court. Most of the houses had children in the family and the kids spent their days riding bikes around the court and visiting each other's homes and backyards. A couple of the houses had pools and many hours were spent swimming and playing. It was a wonderful place to grow up.

Justine and Candice were just under two years apart in age and one year in school. They did most things together growing up. Justine was always the leader and Candice happily followed along with all Justine's ideas. Justine always included Candice when playing with her friends and Candice didn't seem to get in the way. They were each other's first best friends.

Playing school took place in Candice's closet because it was always neat and Justine's was always messy. They'd play *Jem* and sing the songs they heard on the animated TV show on their toy microphone. Justine was always *Jem* and Candice was one of the backup singers. They'd have sleepovers with mutual friends and play Barbie or board games. They especially liked *Monopoly* or *Toronto-opoly* which was a similar game but with local buildings and landmarks. They remained best friends until they were teenagers.

The school was just around the corner, and all the neighbourhood kids walked together to and from school. Justine made many friends and she kept many of them into adulthood. She loved school and her teachers. Her kindergarten teacher had taught

Justine's dad too so that was funny. When Justine was in grade one she loved her teacher so much that she decided she wanted to be a teacher when she grew up. She had decided that she equally loved swimming lessons so her plan was to teach school from Monday to Friday and teach swimming lessons on the weekends. I used to laugh and tell her she would change her mind when she was older and want weekends off to relax but she was adamant that she would want to work seven days a week. She didn't become a teacher or a swimming instructor but she did foresee the future.

Her first brush with fame came when Justine was in grade three. She was given an assignment to write a speech for the public speaking contest. I asked her what she would like to talk about and she immediately said she wanted to do her speech on the topic "Be Careful What You Wish For." I was quite surprised that she chose such a mature topic but she and I wrote a speech, and she practiced and practiced it using lots of expression. She won the public speaking contest for her age group at her school, and she was entered in the contest at the local legion. She won that one too and went on to another legion where she placed second. We knew then that she was destined to be in the limelight. She was a natural.

Justine loved unicorns. She chose pastel coloured unicorn wallpaper border for her bedroom when we gave her a choice of theme. She collected unicorns and had many. *My Little Pony* was a favourite, and she had a unicorn one. *Beanie Babies* were popular and she had a unicorn one. We got her figurines and statues of unicorns for birthdays and Christmas for several years.

Justine got good grades and continued to thrive in her early school and social life. She made many friends and she loved to laugh. There were many birthday parties and camping trips. She even got a paper route and started making some money. Things seemed to be going well until the day that our world crashed down around us. Until the day that changed everything.

THE BOY NEXT DOOR

O ur next door neighbours were the Douglas family. They had moved in a few years after we did. Joan and Peter were the parents and they had three boys. At the time we moved away, Sam was fourteen, James was eleven and Danny was the same age as Justine, seven. Joan babysat and I was thrilled when I found out she would look after my kids. The kids could walk to school and home with the neighbourhood kids and she would look after them until either Greg or I got home from work. The kids liked going to Joan's home. She played with them and they liked the boys. There were other children there to play with too. She was so conveniently close, and it was comforting to know they were right next door.

A couple of times if I went out in the evenings, Sam would come over to babysit at our house if Greg was working the afternoon shift. I liked that his mom was next door in case there might be an emergency. He could just call her to come over to help him. He was a quiet boy but seemed responsible, although I never really saw him take much of an interest in the children. What fourteen year-old boy likes children really anyway?

One time when I was going out, I told Justine that Sam would be babysitting. She said she didn't want him to babysit. I had been working with some high-risk girls at school, and one girl had confided that she had been abused. When Justine told me she didn't want Sam babysitting, my hair stood on end. Had he hurt her? I tried to stay calm. Was I projecting what was going on at work onto this situation? I needed to find out why she didn't want him to babysit. She had been trained so well at school to tell if anyone hurt her. I knew I would get the truth from her. I calmly asked, "Why don't you want Sam to babysit you?"

She shrugged and answered, "I just don't want him to."

I was on high alert and ready to hear the worst. I tried again in a very calm voice, "But why? Did he hurt you?"

She immediately went on the defensive and adamantly stated, "No!"

Phew! I was so relieved. Thank God! I asked again just to be absolutely sure.

"Justine, I need to know why you don't want Sam to babysit. Did he hurt you or touch you inappropriately?" Again her answer was an emphatic, "No!"

"Well, you need to give me a reason because I'm leaving soon," I said. She said she just didn't want him to babysit.

I replied, "I'm sorry you don't want him to babysit but unless you give me a reason, he's coming over in a few minutes and I'm going out." She had no reason, and he came over to babysit. He came maybe three times in total, since we moved soon after that.

She really seemed to like him, and one time as he was walking past our house,

She called out, "Hi, Sam!"

He looked embarrassed and shy and mumbled, "Hi, Justine."

He was fourteen and she was six so he didn't really want to be seen speaking to a little girl. He scurried away. I'm sure that's the last time I saw him.

At the end of Justine's first grade we moved from the city to a small hamlet a half hour away. The kids were sad to leave the neighbourhood and all their friends but some of the families had already moved. It was time to move on. Justine cried all the way to the new house. My heart was broken for her, even though I knew she would like living in a village and would meet many new friends. I felt safer raising my family in a small town and I liked that they would take a bus to school. Our new house had a playground sized swing and slide and a tree fort in the huge yard and I knew Justine would be happy.

Settling into her new school and neighbourhood was easy for such a social girl. She joined Girl Guides, the local soccer team and enjoyed playing with the children in the village. Since her school was out of town she made many friends that did not live within walking distance. I would drive her to play with them and she kept in touch with her friends from the old neighbourhood too. They would have many sleepovers at each other's houses.

Justine loved to swim. I had taken her to a water babies' class when she was a few months old and she had no fear of water. She took swimming lessons every season and continued to pass to the next level. She achieved Bronze Cross at the end of her swimming career and I really thought she might become a lifeguard or swimming instructor as she had planned. She loved to swim for pleasure and spent many hours at the local swimming pool and at the lake when we visited or rented a cottage. Water was extremely important to her.

The day our lives fell apart was two years later. Greg was on afternoon shift. The kids were still at school when I drove up the driveway and saw Greg standing, waiting for me. His face was as white as a sheet. He looked shaken and he was trembling. He looked as if he had very bad news. I braced myself for what he was about to tell me.

"What's wrong?" I asked with great reluctance as I stared up at him from the car window.

His answer was that he had been hanging curtains in Justine's bedroom when her diary fell on the floor. She was eight years old and he thought he would read some cute childlike antics in there so he began reading. The first thing he read was, "I had six with Sam." He and I both knew six was not a number. I was devastated, as any mother would be, but I was also so angry that I had not probed deeper and gotten the truth out of her earlier. Why hadn't all her training worked? Why had she not told? Why had she kept it a secret when I specifically asked her? Why had she just carried on without giving us any inkling this had happened to her?

I didn't know what to do so I called the Rape Crisis Centre. I told them about what she wrote and how I had had an earlier suspicion. I told the counsellor on the phone I didn't want this to be a secret and that I wanted other mothers to realize that they are not immune to their children keeping this horrible secret despite all their training in finding someone they trust and telling them. I was so confident she would have told me. Specifically, I knew she would not lie when I asked her. The woman on the phone said something I will never forget.

She said, "You might not want it kept secret and you might want to tell others, but this is not your story to tell." She went on to say that this is Justine's story to talk about. She advised me to call Children's Aid Society. By the time Justine came home from school, I had talked to several people and had set up a meeting with a social worker at the CAS.

What happened next is something I was not at all prepared for. Greg and I had decided to tell her that I had read the diary. We thought she might accept that better. We thought she would forgive me easier. When she got home from school, I told her I had something to tell her. I told her I read her diary. She screamed and cried and then she ran down to the basement. She was like a wild animal. She was so hurt. She felt so betrayed. She thrashed and pushed me and screamed at me. She had never, ever acted that way before. She hated me!

I was completely crushed. I had just found out my child had been abused and now that child hated me and mistrusted me. I crumpled to the floor, sobbing uncontrollably. Justine was screaming and screaming! It was a very horrifying scene. Candice, who was six, witnessed the entire thing. She had no idea what was going on and she was traumatized.

She asked, "Mommy, why are you crying?"

I answered, "Someone hurt Justine and when someone hurts her, it hurts me too!"

I wanted to include her in what was happening. I had a feeling this would affect her life in a profound way and I wanted to be as honest as I could be. My perfect little family was living a nightmare.

MIDDLE YEARS

I'll never forget the horrifying feeling I had as I took my child into a busy mall, walked up the stairs and entered a door that read "Children's Aid Society". To me, the CAS was for families where the parents hadn't done well. I had to admit to myself that this was me. I was given a child to protect and not allow any harm to come to her. I failed. My family was now involved in the Children's Aid Society. As hard as I tried to not dwell, that fact haunted me.

A social worker took Justine to her group therapy while I was ushered into an office with another social worker. I burst into tears from shame and embarrassment. The male social worker was extremely sympathetic. He tried to explain that I had done the best I could. I've told myself that a million times since then. I did do the best I could. I thought I had chosen someone reliable who could access his mother from right next door. I tried to keep my shame hidden for Justine's sake. I didn't want her to feel any shame for one second. She didn't do anything wrong. I never wanted her to feel she did anything wrong. And I did the best I could.

Justine and I made that same trek for ten sessions and each time as I was climbing the stairs I hoped no one I knew was there to see where I was going. I hoped that the group therapy would help Justine. I'm sure it did. She was always able to talk about what happened and after the initial shock of finding out I read her diary, she forgave me and was always happy that she didn't have to keep that awful secret anymore. She knew it was a blessing that we found out and she likely even wrote that in her diary hoping someone would learn what happened.

Because we had moved away and there was no chance of her ever having to see Sam again, we were dropped from the CAS caseload after the ten sessions and we were able to try to go on with our lives.

Justine seemed to adjust very well. She had coped since it happened and there didn't seem to be any ill effects. She continued to get good grades, have fun with her friends and enjoy a variety of extra-curricular activities. She was involved in her church after-school program, was an altar server, got a solo in the school production of *Joseph and the Technicolour Dream Coat* and was happy.

There were many happy times during those years.

When Justine was in Grade 2, we got a Shih Tzu puppy. The kids named her Taco because she had reddish-brown hair, and they thought it was the colour of taco filling. Since she was a female and my Italian brother-in-law informed me a name ending in o means a male name, we added Belle as her second name. We had Taco Belle for seventeen years. She grew up with the kids, and we had her for a few years after they grew up and got places of their own.

Our family rented a cottage at a small resort every summer during that time. The same families rented at the same time, and all the kids looked forward to spending the week with their friends. It was a fun place, where the kids could swim, fish, and play all day. Justine loved tubing, waterskiing, and trying new things. One day while the kids were swimming in the lake, someone got an inner tube. They were all diving in and out of it and frolicking with it. Justine decided to dive into the tube from the top. I was watching the kids and noticed her feet sticking out of the top while her head was underwater. She was stuck. I alerted everyone, and we jumped in to try to pull her out or try to tip the tube up so she could breathe. It seemed impossible. The tube would not tip since her body was keeping it stabilized, and she was very stuck. I'm not sure how long it took us to free her, but it seemed like forever.

I'm not even sure how she finally got out, whether she was pushed through or how she finally surfaced. This was her third near-death experience.

My daughter had always had strong convictions about environmental issues. We only used non-chemical cleaners, had "garbage-less" lunches, before they were the norm. We were surprised however when one day she decided she wanted to be a vegetarian. She was eight or nine at the time and we thought it was cute, but we dismissed such a silly notion. She would occasionally bring it up and I told her when she grew up she could do whatever she wanted. One Sunday after I had prepared a roast-beef dinner with all the trimmings, Justine sat down at the table and announced she wasn't eating. I asked if she felt sick, but she was very rude, pushed her plate away and stated she wasn't eating "this." Her dad was very firm when he explained she was not to be disrespectful, that her mother had made her a lovely meal and she would eat it. Justine stood up and said she would *not*! She ran into her bedroom and slammed the door. What had just happened? After she cooled down and was able to explain, she said she had decided to be a vegetarian and nothing would stop her. I immediately made a doctor's appointment. I knew he would tell her how unhealthy her decision was and that she was too young to make a decision like that. Our family doctor practiced Eastern medicine as well as Western medicine. He had an acupuncture clinic too. He explained that many cultures and religions practice vegetarianism from birth and that Justine could get all the protein she needed from vegetables, eggs, beans, lentils, nuts, tofu, and cheese. Justine never ate meat ever again. She was ten years old.

Justine was always excited to attend Girl Guide camp. They camped in spring and winter with her pack and spent a week in Haliburton at an overnight camp every summer. One winter they went to Camp Samac for the weekend. I dropped her off on Friday night and planned to spend a relaxing weekend in my pyjamas. At ten o'clock on Saturday morning, I got a phone call. It was the Guide leader. Justine had been taken to the hospital in an ambulance. She had tobogganed down a set of stairs in a "flying saucer" and slammed into a tree. I rushed up to the hospital to find out she had broken her ankle. It was winter and getting around on crutches with a cast is not easy. The next few months were spent driving her to and from school, to doctor appointments and to physiotherapy. Her classroom was an outdoor portable that year and she needed help getting in and out of the classroom and back and forth across a slippery, wooden ramp through the school and across the parking lot in snow and ice. Keeping her plaster cast dry was a nearly impossible feat. We were very happy when she was able to wear an air-filled plastic walking cast. I won't call this a near-death experience, but it could have been more serious than it was. She could have hit her head instead of her leg. Those "toys" are very dangerous. Choosing to go down a set of stairs was reckless. This was just one episode of Justine beginning to make some poor choices.

WINGHAM

Justine loved her extended family. She wrote this speech when she was in Grade four. This speech not the one that won her a place at the Legion Public Speaking contest, but it shows how much she loved going to her grandparents' house for holidays.

MY FAVOURITE PLACE

Yes! We are going to Wingham. Hello teachers, judges and fellow students. My speech this year is about something very special to me. My grandparents' house.

Now I guess you're wondering what Wingham is. It's a small town 150 miles from here. 3000 people live there. I know that sounds like a lot of people but really it isn't. My grandparents lived there for 28 years.

For fun, my cousins and I played hide and seek for hours. There were great hiding places because the house was so big. If there was a good hiding spot, we found it. Another thing we loved to do was ride our bikes around the big circular driveway. I remember when my grandpa went downtown to buy me a bike when I was four or five years old. He asked me what colour I wanted and I said green. He came back with an orange one and I was disappointed. My grandmother tried to make it up me by giving me a green jellybean and I don't even like green jellybeans.

In the summer, we would walk to the park and make good use of the public swimming pool. My favorite part of going to Wingham was that my sister and cousins could walk all over town. It's not that we can't walk around in Hampton, it's just there's nowhere to go. My parents would never let me go to the show by myself, but there we could. There are lots of stores to walk to so we could buy candy.

I speak for all my cousins when I say that our clubhouse was the best. It was three concrete walls and dirt. It led into a valley and into town. We would go on nature walks and find rusty things and stuff like that.

My favorite holiday is Christmas. On Christmas Eve at my grandparents' place, all the cousins gather around and my aunt reads, "The Night before Christmas." Then everybody picks a chair. I guess you were wondering why we pick a chair. Well, we get gifts from Santa and he puts all the gifts on the chair. If we didn't pick a chair, we wouldn't know what gifts would be ours.

One thing I didn't like about Wingham was the three-hour drive. One time my dad said he would take a shortcut and it took us five hours.

This past June, my grandpa died. We will miss him very much and will miss going to Wingham. The big old house is too big for grandma so she moved. But we will always have the memories of going to Wingham.

This speech is a wonderful example of Justine's heart and humor. I especially liked re-reading the part where she describes the clubhouse. Three concrete walls and dirt. It was the composter! The kids sure had fun there and this speech really captures it from a child's point of view.

JUSTINE AND HER GRANDPA

Justine was ten years old when my father died, and Justine, Candice and her cousins were all witness to it. We were all at his big, old house that Justine loved. It was Canada Day weekend. My dad was barbecuing and he and went into the house to get a knife and never came back out again. He had a heart attack in the back porch while we waited for him to return with the steak knife. As you can imagine, it was quite a frantic scene when my mother discovered him lying on the floor. I'll never forget Justine, Candice, and my nephews Eric and Matt all lining the big staircase peering down at the bedlam below.

Justine wanted to speak at her grandpa's funeral, and she was already an award-winning public speaker at that age.

Here is her handwritten eulogy.

Grampa was the nicest person I new. I loved him, everyone did! He always spoiled us kids. He had everything he wanted in life. He led a happy life. Grampa made lots of flower beds. Grampa had lots of friends. I don't think I never, ever saw a frown on his face. I don't think I was ever mad at him. I don't want to say good-bye but I guess I have to. Good-bye Grampa! I love you! Love, Justine

THE WONDER YEARS

J ustine started smoking when she was in grade seven. That might seem a fairly normal rebellious thing for a thirteen-year old to do. It was not normal for Justine. She was a very strong anti-smoking advocate and had been a vegetarian since age ten. She was a strong voice in getting her dad to stop smoking after he had smoked for twenty years. No one ever expected her to start this habit. She began making very poor decisions about other things too. She had always been such a smart, trustworthy daughter and suddenly she was just not to be trusted to use good judgement. Justine was my first child and I knew many kids went through a difficult phase so I just thought she would soon outgrow this phase.

When Justine won the public-speaking contest, we really knew she was good at getting up and speaking in front of people. She had natural confidence and was good at expressing herself. She began auditioning for the school productions which were quite theatrical endeavours for an elementary school. Her school was very fortunate to have a very talented family who directed and provided all the music. They got high school theatre venues for the productions too. Justine really wanted the part of Dorothy in *The Wizard of Oz* and she landed it. She would do half the productions and another girl would do the other half. She had had great success in previous performances and she even sang a solo in *Joseph and the Amazing Technicolour Dreamcoat*. But this was the big time. She went to all the practices, and we were so proud of her.

One day I got a call from the director. She said she was going to have to terminate Justine from the play. I was stunned! It seems Justine was not remembering her lines and it just wasn't working out. I couldn't believe it! When I asked Justine, she said she didn't want to be in the play. I could not understand it after wanting it so much. She just had decided she wanted out. This was a huge red flag that something was terribly wrong.

That New Year's, I got a great scare. Justine's friend had invited her for New Year's Eve and a sleepover. I was not comfortable with it because one time I had gone to pick her up at this friend's house after a sleepover and the parents had no idea where the girls were. I was horrified! How could you not know where your thirteen-year-old daughter was? They lived in a townhouse complex, so I drove around looking for them. They were wandering around with some boys and I was not very happy. I had a very bad feeling about allowing her to stay over on

New Year's Eve so I said no. There was a lot of screaming, begging, and crying but I stood my ground. She ran into her room and slammed the door. Oh well, better for her to hate me than be in an unsafe situation, I rationalized. After an hour or so, I thought maybe she would be calm enough to talk about it. I knocked on her door. No answer. Maybe she was sleeping? I opened the door, and the room was empty! She had snuck out of the house and had begun walking to her friend's place in frigid weather. Her friend lived eleven kilometers away. I jumped in the car and found her just outside of town. I was furious, and she eventually got into the car after a little protest. It was really cold!

One day I got a call from her male teacher. He said he felt uncomfortable with what Justine wore to school. I also felt uncomfortable and every morning ended in a screaming match because Justine dressed very inappropriately. She favoured "spaghetti-strapped" tank tops, and they were very tight and revealing. I sometimes won the battle in the morning, but more often, she stormed off wearing what she wanted. When her teacher called, I knew I had to take more control but I honestly didn't know what to do. She was so strong willed and I knew I had to pick my battles carefully. The more I said, the more she rebelled. I knew that once high school started, things would be better because she had chosen to go to a school that required a uniform. Wishful thinking on my part. What she wore turned out to be the least of our worries.

HIGH SCHOOL

High school started out very well for Justine. She met some new friends and was really applying herself in her schoolwork. She and one of her new friends teamed up for a Shakespearean project. They decided to record a video at the girl's house. Her parents had a canopy bed and Justine was going to recite a scene from *Romeo and Juliet*. I had an old prom dress from the seventies that was perfect for her costume. It had "leg 'o mutton" sleeves and it fit her perfectly. The girl's older brother took the video and it turned out beautifully. They got a really good mark. After *The Wizard of Oz* fiasco, I was happy to see Justine excelling in acting again. I was very optimistic about how things were going.

It was easy to overlook the troubling times because things would go so well for her at other times. Sometimes I would wonder if I was just being an overprotective mother. I really wanted her to be happy and have fun.

I started allowing her to go out more and to sleep over at her new friends' homes. One day she made plans to go to the carnival and stay overnight at her friend's house. I drove the girls to the fair, which was a midway set up in a parking lot of the community centre. Good, clean fun! The girl's parents would pick them up. I went to bed feeling good about allowing Justine to have some fun. At midnight I got a phone call. I was sound asleep when the phone rang. It is never comforting to be awakened by the telephone ringing, but it is particularly disconcerting when you have teenagers. It was the call that no parent wants to receive while trying to clear your mind from a deep sleep. It was the hospital. Justine had been admitted. I better get there. She was unconscious.

Now, we were in a dilemma. Candice had invited her friends over for a sleepover party. Do I call their parents and have the parents come to get their child? Do I leave them alone all night? I had no idea what to expect at the hospital. What would they tell their parents in the morning? These questions flashed through my mind at a furious rate. They were still awake, so I just decided to ask them. They chose staying together all night with no parents at home. They were twelve or thirteen and very responsible. I made them lock all doors and off we went.

When we arrived at the hospital, we got the report that they had pumped Justine's stomach so she didn't die from alcohol poisoning. It was still a very serious time. We spent a very frightening night at the hospital, waiting and hoping she would come out of her coma. When she did in the morning, she apologized. We got the story afterward.

They had left the midway and crossed the street to the ravine where a party had been planned. Justine had passed out and luckily the kids had enough sense to take her to the hospital. She had been literally dropped off at the hospital and the kids sped away in a car. I was always very thankful they had the sense to do that. They could have just left her in the forest. This was yet another near-death experience.

Another one was soon to follow. Justine didn't come home one night. We were frantic with worry. I called everyone I knew to ask if she was there, but no one knew where she was. Again, you have to remember this was before cell phones and I had no way to reach her. We mistakenly thought we had to wait twenty-four hours before contacting the police. It seems we watch too many American police shows. The second the twenty-four hours was up, we were at the police station. That's when they told us we should have come in hours earlier. We filled out a missing person's report and headed home. Within an hour, Justine appeared. She looked disheveled. When we asked where she had been all night,

She said, "In the forest."

This was not the ravine where she had her alcohol-poisoning episode. This was the forest right beside our house. She would not tell us much more and would not tell us whom she had been with. We had our suspicions, however, because she thought she was keeping her boyfriend secret, but we knew. We even had invited him over for dinner, hoping that might scare him away. Justine would only say he was a friend. This boy was several years older than Justine was and had been having a few problems of his own. We would have been much happier if she would admit she was seeing him so we could keep tabs on them. She said later that she knew we would never approve of their relationship, so she kept it secret. She knew he was not good for her and eventually they broke up. They remained friends.

Other troubling signs were beginning to appear. One day I noticed some red marks on Justine's wrists. I asked to see them and she was very reluctant to show me. I eventually convinced her to show me. There were a series of cut marks on her arm. I was extremely alarmed. Had she tried to slit her wrists? I began trying to find out what had happened. She told me she was not trying to commit suicide. She had used a utility knife to cut into her flesh. She explained that it made her feel better. I was completely shocked. How could hurting yourself make you feel better? She said it released the pain. I had never heard of "cutting" before. I was completely baffled and felt the need to seek help for her. I had no idea where I would turn for such help. Justine shrugged it off and started getting ready for work. She wore a short-sleeved shirt to work. I tried to convince her to call into work and tell them she couldn't come. How could she go to work with slash marks on her arm? She would not hear of it. I did manage to bandage it up and off she went to work as a hostess of a restaurant. I asked her at the end of the shift if anyone had mentioned the bandage and she said no one mentioned anything.

By this time, I knew I needed to find out how to get her some psychiatric help. I had no idea where to begin. Someone suggested I see my medical doctor and he could tell me what to do. His suggestion was to take her to the crisis clinic. I had never heard of it before and had no idea what to do. He explained that it was in the emergency department of the hospital. This was the beginning of hours and hours of waiting in the emergency waiting room of the hospital for the next several years. And those were only for the times she would agree to go. The first time was a real eye opener. She was not very willing to go, but I begged her and she reluctantly agreed. Spending hours and hours in a hospital waiting room is no fun for anyone. When they finally called her name, they sent us upstairs to the psychiatric department. We waited in that waiting room for an hour or so before they called her name. We both stood up to go into the office. I was immediately stopped and told I couldn't go with her. I explained that I'm her mother. I was told that confidentiality is paramount. We spent hours at psychiatrists, psychologists, therapists and counsellors. I was not welcome nor did I ask any questions. They refused to answer any if I asked. When she came out of the office twenty minutes later, she had a white piece of paper in her hand. I asked what it was, and she showed me. It was a prescription for Paxil. I was horrified. I brought her there to get help, not drugs. I soon learned that that was the only "help" they offer at the crisis clinic.

We would visit the crisis clinic many more times, however. Justine would take the medication and we would monitor how she felt and if it was helping her. She really would give it several months, but eventually she would want to get off it. We would try another one and another one, but the side effects were awful and Justine hated them. She eventually decided to go off them altogether. She said she didn't feel like herself when she was on them. We certainly didn't want her to lose her identity, but we did see a difference in her while she took them. She didn't scream or cry and it seemed to calm her.

Even though she went to school, she didn't necessarily attend class. I got one very troubling phone call that Justine was found sleeping on the bench in the hallway at school one day. The vice principal said they couldn't allow her to do that. No kidding! I was mortified. At this time, we knew she suffered from depression and there would be days she could not function. She would stay in bed or sleep on the couch all day. I would let her sleep for a while but then prod her and badger her to get up. She sometimes would groggily get up and I would take her to school. I didn't know what else to do at times like these. I had to get to work and I was afraid to leave her home alone. We needed help and we weren't getting any by sitting for hours in the hospital waiting room and leaving with a prescription Justine wouldn't take.

We were stunned from the beginning that Justine was not referred to a counsellor or therapist. We were told that the psychiatric department isn't connected with this type of therapy. It's separate. The psychiatrists we see on television are not the type we encountered. There was no couch to lie on and they certainly didn't take any time to listen to any problems. Writing prescriptions seemed to be their only job. I honestly forget how I finally got her into a program, but it took much navigating and many phone calls. The system is definitely not friendly.

Justine was very eager to find someone she could talk to. Why was it so difficult to find someone? Finally we found Susan. She was a counsellor for children and teenagers. Justine loved her! She looked forward to her appointments and she felt it really helped her. She continued seeing Susan on a regular basis for four years.

Justine was scheduled to meet with Susan one of the times she overdosed. I tried to wake her up, but she seemed groggier than usual. When I finally got her to sit up, I could see her eyes were foggy and I feared the worst. I checked her prescription and it was half empty. She was coherent and agreed to get up and shower for her appointment. I wanted Susan to see her and realize she needed more help than we were providing. Justine staggered into the shower and I heard a crash! She fell! I know now I should have called an ambulance, but when you live with crisis every day, it becomes "normal" and I felt confident Susan would know what to do. I think I may have showered her myself although I can't remember. I know I got her to her appointment and watched her stagger into Susan's office. I had never been allowed to go with her into the office, but this time they called me in. Susan said she thought Justine had taken too many pills. I said I had suspected that, but didn't know what to do. We needed help! Her solution? Go to the hospital crisis clinic.

We were going round and round and round but this was my only recourse. I really hoped that this visit would be different since she had actually taken too many pills so maybe they would admit her. We sat for hours in the waiting room, as usual. I was left in charge of monitoring her. When her turn came, we went upstairs and waited up there, as usual. When she came out of the office, she was carrying yet another prescription. I was livid. I demanded to talk to the psychiatrist. We were left waiting for another long while before I was finally ushered in. I told him what had happened. Had she mentioned she had overdosed? Did he have any suggestions for us? We needed help! He said he could not discuss his patient with me because of confidentiality and dismissed me. We went home not one bit wiser or having received any help. From then on, I kept Justine's pills beside my bed and doled them out myself.

The second time Justine attempted to overdose, we took more action. She had wanted to go somewhere or do something we felt was unsafe so we said she couldn't go. I can't remember all the details, but she didn't like our answer. She began screaming, ran into my room, grabbed her pills and locked herself in the bathroom. Greg got a key and tried to get in, but the bathroom is designed so that she could lodge herself between the vanity and the wall and completely block the door. We tried frantically to convince her to open the door. She screamed she was going to kill herself. I called 911. When a police constable came to the door, we explained that we didn't know what else to do. He said we did the right thing. An ambulance arrived shortly after and by then she had opened the door. They put her on a stretcher and took her to the hospital by ambulance. Her third ambulance ride and yet another near-death experience.

HOSPITAL

The hospital finally decided to admit Justine after reviewing her records and given the fact she arrived by ambulance. They put her in the psychiatric ward. Since she was 16, she went into the adult ward. She seemed to settle in surprisingly well. She made friends with many of the patients and sometimes when I would visit it appeared to be almost a party-like atmosphere. Many of the patients smoked and although there were signs warning them not to drink coffee, many of them, including Justine, would go downstairs and buy a large coffee at the coffee shop and spend much of their day out on the terrace with coffee and smokes. It was December and it was winter in Canada, but they didn't seem to mind the cold.

There were many memorable characters in the psychiatric ward. One man was Indigenous and had long black hair. He appeared to be thirty-five to forty years old. The first time I went to see Justine I saw him sitting in the dining area with his head hanging in his dinner. He was a big man and I have to admit I felt a little frightened that he and other men were sharing a ward with my sixteen year-old daughter. The nurses only appeared at med times and for the rest of the day they stayed behind the nurses' station. I hoped they had cameras watching the patients, but to me, it seemed there was no supervision. I wondered who was looking out for my daughter.

The next day I arrived and couldn't find Justine. I asked around and someone said she was in the TV room. When I located her she was sitting with Garth. I was shocked to find the two of them alone in such a secluded area. When Justine saw me she said goodbye to Garth and came with me. She could hardly wait to tell me about Garth. It seemed they had developed quite a friendship. She said he was the most interesting man she'd ever met. Although I was happy that she seemed to be getting better and was much happier than I had seen her in a long time, I was taken aback that her new best friend seemed to be right out of *One Flew over the Cuckoo's Nest*.

The following day I found her with him again, only this time he looked completely different. Justine had convinced him to let her wash and cut his hair! She had snipped off his pony tail with the intention of donating it to kids with cancer. It seems they were spending all their time together. Within a few days, Garth was gone but Justine always looked for him when she was downtown. He was often homeless, and she always wanted to know he was all right. I think one time she did run into him, but he had returned to his drug habit and she didn't think he remembered her or was in no frame of mind to recognize her. Years later, I found Garth's pony tail in Justine's closet. She had kept it.

I visited with Justine every day after work until evening. She also had other visitors. One visiting session was very memorable because of the coffee. Our friends came to visit Justine but didn't really get a chance to see her. Justine had not been sleeping. I think it was partially because she was a teenager and we all know their sleeping patterns are different. Because of the party atmosphere mixed with medications and topped off with gallons of caffeine, Justine had been up many, many hours without sleep. It had finally taken its toll and she was a quivering, screaming mess. Her body was literally shaking off the bed. It was frightening. I felt badly for our friends who came to visit on my recommendation that she was doing so well. They stayed to comfort me for a short while but I felt I needed to be with Justine and to try to see if I could get her to relax and sleep. I just lay with her and held her. Eventually, she began to stop trembling and fell asleep.

Justine stayed for two weeks in the hospital with weekends at home. She was feeling great and the psychiatrist was actually listening to her instead of just doling out prescriptions. She finally felt she was getting the help she so desperately wanted. She made friends with many of the older women too. There was nobody her age there so she socialized with one woman who appeared to be sixty-five and two others who looked to be in their forties. They all had a great camaraderie because they understood each other and finally felt accepted. Sometimes I felt like a real outsider when I was there. I wasn't one of them.

Justine was released the week of Christmas. She felt sad to be leaving her new friends. She really had enjoyed staying there and they were so supportive. Being back in the real world was difficult. She slept a lot and seemed to be sinking back into depression. We usually have at least 10 for Christmas dinner, but that year there, were just seven of us; my sister, her two boys and our family. Justine had not been interacting with her cousins since their arrival and continued to sleep on the couch as they watched movies and conversed. When dinner was served, Justine did not want to come to the table. I insisted she at least sit with us. While at the table, she reminded me of the first time I saw Garth. She sat with her head hanging in her dinner while the rest of us pretended there wasn't an elephant in the room. Greg had a gallbladder attack and went to bed and the dinner was a complete disaster. That was the worst Christmas of my entire life.

The rest of the week was more of the same. Justine was depressed and slept all the time. When New Year's came, she asked if she could spend it with her friends from the hospital. I said no several times before she talked me into letting her go. The party was at a condo downtown and it seemed to be something she really wanted to do. She wanted to reconnect and have a re-union. I was happy she wanted to actually have some fun. I drove her there and would pick her up at one o'clock. At eleven thirty, I got a tearful phone call from Justine asking if I could come and get her. She was outside standing on the street downtown. I was frightened for her safety. This was no place for a teenager to be alone at midnight. I told her to stay there and I raced to go get her before something happened to her. When I got there, there was a police car there. I felt my heart sink. What would they think of my parenting skills allowing my teenage daughter to be out alone downtown at midnight? I explained that she had been at a party, and she had just gotten out of the hospital, I got there as soon as I could, and that everything was fine I would take her home now. I'm sure I sounded like a blathering idiot. The cop asked if I knew why they were there. I said because they were likely worried when they saw a young girl on the street at midnight all alone. He shook his head. He said they had gotten a call from her friends at the party. It seems things had gotten out of hand and Justine had tried to jump off the balcony. Her friends were worried about her and had called the police to go look for her. I'd lost track of how many life threatening-experiences this one was.

MR. BROWN

Most school mornings, it was a big struggle to get Justine out of bed, showered and get to her to eat something for breakfast. I always drove her to school on my way to work so I would be sure she would get there each day. I didn't trust her to get to the bus and feared she would crawl back into bed the minute I left. I know this is a common ritual for most parents of teenagers.

While I was at work one day, I got a message to call Justine's school. Justine was sixteen at the time. I work with teens who have special needs and it is very difficult for me to get to a phone during class time. I called as soon as I could, but I was very concerned. I talked to the secretary and she asked me why Justine wasn't at school. I was immediately very worried. This was before cellphones and I had no idea what happened to her after I watched her walk into the school. I spent all day wondering where she was and what she was doing. Was she at a friend's house? Was she wandering the streets? Was she in trouble? By the time she arrived home at the usual time that day, I was very relieved but also upset and angry. I demanded to know where she had been all day. She told me she had been at school. I told her about the phone call I got in the morning and how I knew she hadn't been at school. She insisted that she had been at school. I wanted to believe her and because I worked in a high school, I knew sometimes the teachers make mistakes or the attendance is already at the office if the student arrives to class late. There was no reason she should have been late because I dropped her off early. I asked if she had arrived late to her home room class and she said she had been talking to Mr. Brown for the period.

Who was Mr. Brown? He was her religion teacher. He encouraged his students who had problems to come and spend his on-call period with him to discuss their personal issues. I was furious with Mr. Brown. How irresponsible of him to talk to kids when they were supposed to be in other classes and not inform the teacher or the office. I had had a very stressful day wondering and worried about my child. The next time I got a phone call (and I got many more), I asked the secretary to check if she was in the school and she always was. In hindsight, I should have gone into the school and informed them of Mr. Brown. Justine asked me not to because she said he was helping her. This would not be the last time Justine would tell me about Mr. Brown.

Exam time arrived and because I worked in a high school, I knew the content of the grade eleven religion curriculum. It was quite intense since it involved religions of the world and there was much to study. Justine refused to study. She told me that Mr. Brown told the class it would be one essay and it would be their own opinion, so they didn't have to study. I had never heard of that kind of exam or a teacher giving that kind of advice, and I still encouraged her to study since I thought that the different religions would need to be understood in order to write an intelligent essay. She adamantly refused to study despite my pleading and reasoning. I expected her to return home after that exam crying. I knew she would most likely fail the exam. She came home very happy and confident she had done very well. I was doubtful.

When she got her exam results, Justine came home with an "I told you so" attitude. She was very saucy when she bragged about the mark she got on her exam. The exam was an opinion exam and as long as the students could support their opinion, they passed. Justine had no problem supporting any opinion she had about anything. She got 100 percent on the exam. I had never heard of a student getting 100 percent unless he or she was extremely smart and an exception. Most times, a spelling mistake or some other error would result in losing a mark or two. Justine was a notoriously bad speller. She was educated during a time when whole language and content was encouraged and spelling errors were overlooked. Again, I felt Mr. Brown undermined my authority as a parent.

Mr. Brown 2
Mom 0
One day, a year or two later, while I was in the staff room of the school I worked in, I was telling that story to some of my colleagues. The teachers were listening intently because of the liberties Mr. Brown had taken with the content of the exam and with the unusually high mark she was awarded. I was still stinging from losing the respect of my sixteen year-old daughter when I so desperately needed it. A teacher I had never seen before who had been sitting at another table came over after overhearing my story. He said he'd given students 100 percent on exams many times. After he left, I asked the other teachers if they knew who that man was. They told me he was the new religion teacher, Mr. Brown.

This would not be the last time we would run into Mr. Brown. Years later, while Justine was working part-time at a large chain hardware store, she came home and asked me to guess who started working in her store. It was, you guessed it, Mr. Brown. I had heard of people who had retired getting a part-time job at this store, but I was still surprised to hear that a retired teacher was working there. I was also a little concerned he was working with my daughter. Although I had no proof of any impropriety on his part during that time when he was having private talks with Justine, I knew she had been vulnerable and he was not a social worker. I always felt uneasy about his motivations and the discussions were obviously carried out in secret. Justine clearly liked him very much for helping her and for that 100 percent mark, of course.

Justine soon began seeing Mr. Brown in a very different light. She began losing respect for him once he wasn't in a position of authority and merely a co-worker. She would come home with stories of Mr. Brown behaving "weirdly" at work. Her co-workers were beginning to talk. Justine soon learned the truth. Mr. Brown had been taking breaks in his car and drinking on the job. He was drunk at work. It wasn't long before Mr. Brown was fired.

PARTIES

When I was a teenager, we used to have a lot of parties. I wanted my kids to have fun too. I had a birthday party each year for my kids. I even took a cake-decorating course so I could learn to make designer cakes. Each year I would ask them what theme they wanted and I would rent the pan and make a cute cake. When Justine was turning six, I asked her what cake she wanted. She said, "Could I have a cake from the grocery store?" That ended my cake making days. She chose one from the grocery store every year after that.

When she graduated from grade eight, she asked if she could have a grad party. We have a big back yard so I told her we could have it outside, and she could invite the whole class. We set up tables outside and put out food and drinks. We planned to have a campfire later in the evening. Greg and I stayed in the house at her request. We did keep peeking out the window to make sure things were OK. At one point, all the kids came in the house and I had to suggest they go back outside and we would start the bonfire. They were getting bored. We went out to start the fire and they all scattered. There were only a few kids left. They didn't go home because only a couple of them lived within walking distance. I tried to find them, but some had run into the forest beside our house and a few ran down the street. I was very upset. When their parents came to pick them up, I had to admit they had run away. I was mortified. They hadn't gone far, but I told Justine that was the last party she would be having for such a big crowd.

Another party stands out in my mind. She was invited to a party in a house in the country. I did not know the girl or her parents so I called to make sure they would be home. They told me they would be there to supervise. Justine was fifteen. Another parent was driving the kids there and I was picking them up. When the time came, I drove there and knocked on the door. The music was blasting and I asked for Justine and her friend. Someone said they'd be right out. I went to the car to wait. A few minutes later, Justine came wobbling out of the door and staggered right off the end of the porch. She was drunk. I couldn't believe my eyes. I ran out of the car to help her up and get her into the car. I was concerned, but also angry.

I said, "I thought the parents were going to be home supervising the party."

She slurred her answer. "They were there! They were so much fun! They were drinking with everyone!" So much for responsible parenting. My first clue should have been the beer cases that lined the outside brick wall. They were about six feet high.

One other party turned out to be very memorable. Justine had invited some friends for a hot tub party and sleepover. She was about eighteen. I was home but they didn't need any supervision. Greg was working overnight and I just stayed in my bedroom watching TV so they could watch movies in the family room and use the hot tub on the deck. I fell asleep and woke up to the sound of the doorbell ringing and knocking on the front door. I waited for the girls to answer it, but it continued. I was annoyed because I was awakened and I could hear the girls were still awake and not bothering to answer. I finally dragged myself up and went to the door. A very stoned Goth boy was weaving in front of me. I thought that if I just gently nudged him he might fall over. I felt a little sorry for him. He looked pathetic.

I said, "The girls are in the back. I'll see if they want you to join them."

He perked up slightly and asked to use the washroom. I said, "Sure," and pointed him toward the bathroom. I went into the family room to tell the girls off for not answering the door and making me get up. I told them a guy was at the door.

Justine said, "Was it a guy with black hair?"

I answered, "Yes." They all screeched.

Justine said, "Did you get rid of him?" I told them that he was in the bathroom. Justine ran to the washroom and listened at the door.

She said, "I think he's in the shower!"

"What?" I asked

"Oh," she replied, "he's just washing his hands."

She said, "Get rid of him," and she went to join her friends leaving me responsible for getting a guy out of the house.

When he finally came out of the bathroom, I scooted him toward the door saying, "Sorry, bud. The girls don't want you here." I gently pushed him out the door and locked it. I went back to tell the girls. That's when they told me he had been terrorizing them all night. The girls had been in the hot tub and Justine started getting scared. She said she could see someone in the backyard in the dark. Justine had been known to see things at other times and she did get scared easily. She always thought Sam would find her. He had threatened her and warned her not to tell anyone what he did or he would come after her. She thought she saw him at school one day at recess and I got a call that she was hysterical. The girls laughed and thought she was just seeing things. She insisted she could see someone watching them. Sure enough, they saw him too! They all screamed, and ran into the house and locked the patio door. He came up onto the deck and knocked on the door. He was peeking in. They were really scared. He went away for a while and returned to the front door where I let him in. I looked out the window and realized the sun was coming up. It was six o'clock.

Greg arrived home from work an hour later and I told him what had happened. Of course he wasn't too happy with my decision to let a strange boy into the house when he wasn't home. It was difficult to explain that I honestly thought it was around eleven o'clock and that he seemed very harmless. That afternoon as Greg was cutting the lawn, he called for me to go outside. He had found something he wanted me to see. It was a gun lying beside the house. We knew we needed to call the police. Again I had to explain that I had opened the door and invited a strange boy into the house at 5:30 a.m. after he had been spying on my daughter and her friends and terrifying them. Again, I got a scolding. This time from the police. They said that the girls had the right to call the police. The kicker is that this boy's father was chief of police. These guys had to go to their boss's house and explain what his son had been doing all night. I'm quite sure no charges were laid and the gun turned out to be a very realistic-looking pellet gun. Wasn't that a party!

A WORKING GIRL

Justine started her working career at the age of ten. She and her sister shared a paper route. Their dad had a paper route, when he was growing up, and when the opportunity arose for our local paper to be delivered in our neighbourhood, the kids jumped at the chance. It was a great job because it was excellent exercise, they got to know all the neighbours and they made great money. Greg tallied it up once and it was the equivalent of ten dollars an hour which was over the minimum wage at the time.

Justine loved to work.

When a French fry truck opened in town, Justine created her resume, walked down and got herself a job. She was the sole employee of the enterprise. She washed, peeled, cut, and worked the deep fryer. Making change and handling the money were also big responsibilities. She was only thirteen years old at the time. She worked after school some days and all weekend. The owner also owned the pizza parlour, and she would often work there if someone was away. After her shift was over, she was often asked to babysit for the owner and she would not get home some nights until after two in the morning. She loved it.

After two years, the owner sold the business and she had to pound the pavement for a new job. It gave her purpose and kept her busy. She got great satisfaction from earning her own money. She handed out resumes all around the nearby communities and finally landed a hostess job at a chicken franchise. She really wanted to be a server, but she was only fifteen. They told her when she turned sixteen she could apply for a serving position. When she applied a year later, there were no openings.

She decided to look for a server position at some of the other restaurants nearby.

She got a job at a sport bar as a hostess with the promise of working up to server. She worked for almost a year as hostess before she was promoted to server. She was very excited to work as a server because then she would be making tips. She got a copy of the shifts she was expected to work. We drove her for the fifteen minute drive into work the first evening she was scheduled to work as a server. Her shift was four hours long. After the shift, her dad picked her up. He asked how it went. It turned out they had not needed her so she sat doing nothing the entire time. She had missed a social event that evening. Why hadn't she called and had us pick her up? Her manager said she had to stay, so she had to wait to see if business picked up. Then they would have her start. Business was slow that evening. Her dad tried to see the bright side. At least she made some money he rationalized.

"I didn't make a cent!" she cried. "They don't pay me unless I work, and I didn't work."

"What? That can't be right!" her dad said. "That can't be true."

Being an employee of a unionized auto manufacturer, he did not believe a business could treat its employees so shabbily. He called the labour board to find out what to do. The labour board told him that restaurants have the right to do that. We were aghast! We encouraged her to quit and try to get her hostess job back. The restaurant where she worked before had a union and did not treat its employees that way. Besides, it was always busy so there was never any down time to be sitting around. Business was booming there. She had to give two weeks' notice and go in for a few shifts. Then one night near the end of the two weeks, she came out crying. A large table had "dined and dashed," and she had to pick up their tab. She lost money that night after working very hard. The real crime was that she knew the boys who stiffed her. She went to school with them. That experience was heartbreaking for her.

She was again out of work but soon got a job at a large chain hardware store in the paint department. She really enjoyed helping people choose paint and she liked her co-workers. She had fun working there. She worked there for two and a half years until another exciting opportunity at a restaurant as a server was offered to her.

She worked there for a couple of years and really liked serving. She had her regular customers and she liked her coworkers. It was busy, and the time went fast. She worked many hours there because she would cover for people who called in sick, so she worked extra hours. She was still in high school, and this was already her fifth job.

TRUE ROMANCE

Justine had a few long-term romantic relationships. When she worked at the chicken restaurant, she began dating Andrew. When she worked at the hardware store, she began dating one of the managers who worked there. A few years later, she developed a serious relationship with another manager who worked there.

Andrew was Justine's first long-term boyfriend. He was a cook and she was the hostess at a restaurant. Justine was sixteen and he was eighteen. The first time I met him he drove her home from work. He was handsome in a boyish way. He had reddish hair, and was tall and slim. They saw each other at work, and I would drive her over to his place some evenings where they would watch TV and play video games. I don't remember them actually going out very much except to the odd party and the CNE, where he won a big teddy bear with a big red bow for her at one of the games. We still have that teddy bear. The relationship lasted a year or so.

Joe was a little older than Justine and had two children. They also worked together but in different departments. Justine took over the step-mother role quite easily considering she was only eighteen. They spent a lot of time together. When our family would go to the cottage to visit my mom and step-father, Joe would always come with us. He would come for dinner sometimes and we got to know him a little. He did seem to be hard to know, I always thought. One morning, I had forgotten my shirt in the laundry room, and I went in the dark to retrieve it. I was wearing only a bra and my pants. I was not prepared to find Joe waiting at the door to pick Justine up for work. He did have the presence of mind to look down! Justine spent a lot of time at Joe's place. He shared it with his two daughters, his brother, his brother's girlfriend, and their baby girl. Justine became quite close to the whole family and would often come home with stories of what the kids said or what stage the baby was at. Joe was a hard worker, and they dated for a couple of years.

Justine's next serious relationship would come a little later. She met this guy while at the hardware store and they were friends for many years. The circumstances that led to their relationship blossoming are another story.

SHOULD I INCLUDE THIS?

I have wanted to write this story for many years. I really felt it might help other people who are bipolar and those who love them explain what they are going through so that they don't feel alone or so that no one else has experiences like this. Because this is Justine's story, I had always hoped she might give talks on the topic, since she was a great public speaker when she was a child. Maybe we could have written it together. I can't keep wondering "what if." I'm the one who is left now and I know her life story is worth telling.

When I finally decided to write, I told my family I would not sugar coat what happened. Everyone was supportive. Mental illness has been hidden in the shadows for too long. Unless we discuss what we are going through, the stigma will remain. We have to talk about this and that includes some not-so-nice things. This next episode is one of the not-so-nice stories.

One Friday night when Justine was fifteen, she went over to her friend's house for the evening. I felt fairly content since she was in town and not staying overnight. We agreed I would pick her up at midnight. At nine o'clock, she called to say she was fine and that they were watching movies. A couple of hours later I got a knock on my door. I looked out and saw a police car idling in my driveway. I was surprised, but not worried since I knew where Justine was and she was safe. It never occurred to me that the police would be there for anything concerning Justine. I almost thought they were there to ask me if I'd seen anything unusual in the neighbourhood or maybe they had the wrong place. They asked me if I knew Justine Brooks.

"Yes," I reluctantly answered. I told them I was her mother. Why were they asking about Justine? They said they had her in the police car. I was flabbergasted. How did she get in a police car? They said she had been drinking. A woman had called the police when she heard knocking on her door. When she opened the door, there stood a very drunk girl with no pants on. What? What was I hearing? My brain would not compute this information. I ran out to the car and there she was, curled up in the back seat, covered up with a blanket, sleeping. When I got her up, she indeed had no pants on. Where in the world had she lost her pants?

I asked for more information. They had only the information they told me. Fortunately the person's door she had been knocking on was in another town. How they got there I have no idea. How she got separated from her friend is another mystery. When I asked her to tell me what had happened the following day, she had a very vague recollection of going to another town. They began drinking and after that, she blacked out. To this day how, and why she had no pants on haunts me.

Writing this book was sometimes troubling because I often felt a sense of betrayal to Justine. This was her life and exposing some things she might not want people to know about was difficult. Although she was open about her illness, she probably felt embarrassed about some episodes. I struggled with this part, in particular. Is it my embarrassment? Would she want everyone to know? I decided to include it. No sugar coating.

CO-OP

C o-op stands for co-operative education. It's a collaboration between a place of work and school where the employer trains the student and the student earns a high-school credit. When I was in high school, there were no co-op options. However, I did have a work placement that I had permission to go to during school hours. It all started because I was very involved in YACMR, a group of teenagers across Canada who volunteered to work with people who had developmental challenges. The nursery school in town was in need of help and asked me if I would be able to go one morning a week. I asked the principal and he agreed. I didn't receive formal credit for it but I do believe it did help me get accepted into the college program I was interested in.

I always encouraged my children to take co-op. It's such a great opportunity to get hands-on experience while going to school. The students get credit for it just like any other subject, but there is very little homework, no tests, and no studying. Justine had three co-op placements while in high school. Some were more successful than others.

Justine's passion was working with the homeless. She always considered herself one step away from homelessness. She knew that many homeless people have mental health issues and she understood that it could happen to anyone. Her first placement was at the soup kitchen. She always enjoyed serving dinner to the array of characters who came to eat each evening. The philosophy at this kitchen was that each person is worthy of sitting down and being served. There was no lining up for food. Justine and other volunteers would serve the food at the table. She got the opportunity to meet many of the guests and she enjoyed talking with them. She was very successful and often volunteered after the placement was over.

Her next placement was at a shelter for abused women. She found this placement a little more challenging. One day she asked me if she could stay longer and go out with some of the women. I did not think this was a good idea from a professional standpoint. I maintained that people should not socialize with clients they work with. Justine was a teenager and did not really understand that perspective. I was also a little concerned for her safety. I wondered if any of the abusers would find their wife or girlfriend and try to harm them. Justine assured me that they were all from out of town. Another day, Justine's supervisor asked to speak with me. She was concerned about Justine. She said that she was exhibiting some of the same behaviours the women were. This was very troubling. Soon Justine was "fired" from her placement.

I didn't know what to do with this information. Since it was a half-day placement, I was worried about Justine being out of school and idle every afternoon. She had already completed a couple of months so it was too late to enroll her in classes. I met with the supervisor and they agreed she could work at the office for the remainder of the semester. This was a very generous offer. Justine was not in a very good frame of mind, however. This was during the time of multiple trips to the crisis clinic and trying to find the right balance of medication. They called me one day to pick her up because she had curled up on the couch and fallen asleep. I honestly don't remember if she got the credit or not, but she wasn't very successful that year in many subjects.

The following year, Justine's placement was at a drop-in centre for the homeless. It was a storefront downtown a block away from the kitchen where she had worked before. She knew many of the clientele and really liked working there. It was open during the morning and afternoon for breakfast and lunch, although food was not the primary service. There was a doctor, dentist, hairdresser, and other services available as well as clothing and laundry facilities. It was a place to come in out of the cold and socialize too.

During this time, Justine was always on the look-out for her pal, Garth, whom she met at the hospital. She would hear of him from some of the people whom she met every day but never saw him until one day she came home and told me she finally saw him. She was very excited when she saw him but ended up being disappointed. He didn't seem to recognize her or remember her at all. I explained that he was likely under the influence of drugs and alcohol and that she should not take it personally, but I knew she was very hurt. She had wanted to know he had made some positive changes in his life, but it seemed he had just gone back to his old ways. Justine understood this cycle of ups and downs all too well. She had been hoping for a joyful reunion and he didn't even know her. One more heartbreak.

PROM

J ustine did not graduate from her high school. She was one or two credits short and could not concentrate on school work anymore. She also suffered from test anxiety and this caused great stress. She had a job and was happy working so she didn't go back to her high school. I do recall driving her to an alternative high school for a semester, but I'm not sure if she succeeded in attaining all her credits.

She did attend her high school prom though. She had a very specific idea for a short dress and she had it handmade. It was red taffeta with black, shiny trim. She didn't bring a date and told me that I was old fashioned for thinking that one was required. I was happy that people didn't need a date anymore. She met her girlfriend at her house, I took a few pictures and off they went. There was a "field" party afterwards at a farm. She brought a change of clothes and camping gear to spend the night. I was very uneasy about it, but I recall a few bush parties from my own youth and this was prom so I had to let my own fears go.

Early the next morning we got a phone call from a number we did not recognize. It was a woman who asked Greg if Justine was our daughter. Justine had been in their backyard. We got their address and drove to pick her up. Justine said she had gone for a drive with a guy and he tried to assault her so she got out of the car in the middle of nowhere and started walking. Her phone got left behind. We were very relieved that these people invited her into their home and called us. The situation could have been much worse. Rape? Another near-death experience?

ROLL UP THE RIM

We are big coffee drinkers in our family. My mother-in-law always claims she bought one of the first jars of instant coffee ever sold. I have memories of my mother always trying to kick her cream and sugar habit. We've always ground our own beans and made a pot of coffee every day since we've been married. It's no surprise that Justine loved coffee too. There was the episode in the hospital as a low point, but there's also a high point.

Justine was a big fan of Canada's favourite coffee. She would buy several cups a day to keep her fuelled up. Every year Tim Horton has a promotion and it gives away great prizes. The prizes are revealed by rolling up the rim of the coffee cup after the cup is empty. Most of the prizes are a free coffee or donut, but it also gives away cars and bigger prizes too.

One day, Justine rolled up the rim and discovered she had won a forty-six inch plasma TV. This was when plasma TVs were new, and they cost $6,000, so it was a great prize to win. She didn't need a TV and planned to sell it to buy a car. Her dad did not want to see that TV slip through his fingers, so we made a deal. I gave Justine my car, I bought a new one and her dad kept the TV. I was due for a new car anyway and it suited all of us. We still have that TV. It is twelve years old and in perfect working order. Justine had her own car.

BREAKING BAD

It started the very first day of school for both of us. Justine had upgraded some of her marks at an alternative high school and started a marketing course at a private career college. We were very proud of her. The hours at the college suited her perfectly because she was holding down her marketing job and the serving job at the restaurant as well as going to school. I was always trying to convince her to quit one of the jobs but she loved them both. I thought that she was following the plan she'd had since she was a child of being a teacher during the week and a swimming instructor on weekends. I remember laughing at the thought of anyone working seven days a week. I told her she would change her mind when she got older but she stuck with the plan. Now she was adding college to her already full life. I mistakenly believed being so busy would keep her out of trouble.

I was not expecting a phone call my first day back after the summer break. It's difficult to take a call any day while working with students who have special needs but when we're all trying to find classrooms, meeting new teachers and getting to know new students, it's especially disruptive to be called to the phone. It's a little embarrassing too. The teacher has a tough job taking attendance, learning new names, giving out textbooks, and going over the expectations and curriculum. Having the class phone ring in the middle of all that and having to call me out is not something I enjoy. I have to take my student with me, or if there is another educational assistant in the same class, I have to ask if he/she can take on an additional responsibility and watch my student while I leave the classroom. I have to go to the closest phone which in this case was the staff room and have a private conversation in a very public place. During Justine's school life, this had happened more times than I could count. Justine was an adult attending college now. I thought those days were over.

This time it was not her teacher or the vice principal calling. It was Greg. Justine was in jail. What? My heart sunk to my knees. My head exploded. I started to shake. My mouth went dry and tears sprung to my eyes. My heart began pounding so hard I was sure the teachers who were overhearing my conversation could hear it too. Justine had been speeding past an elementary school which was horrifying enough. What was she thinking on the first day of school? Not only could she have hurt a child, there were police watching for people speeding in school zones. People do not get thrown in jail for speeding, however. When the police stopped her, they saw a marijuana "cigarette" in her ashtray. They asked her to open her trunk. She was charged with drug trafficking and put into a holding cell at the police station until we could post bail. I was absolutely stunned. Shaken to the core!

Greg had been enjoying his coffee and newspaper when he got a visitor at the door. The police officer asked him if he knew Justine Brooks. He confirmed he was her father. They told him what happened which was shocking enough. Then they asked to search the house. Greg should have asked for a search warrant, but he was not thinking of his rights at that point. He invited them in and guided them to her bedroom, where they found even more drugs. Greg was then implicated because the drugs were in our home. He thought they might arrest him. They questioned him for what seemed like forever and finally realized he was innocent.

I honestly don't remember what happened after hearing this unbelievable story that was my life. I somehow got through the day. There was no way I was asking to leave early the first day of school and there was really nothing I could do. Greg was arranging to put up our house as collateral for bail money. I was sorry I couldn't be there to support him. I was very angry with Justine and could not believe the bad timing.

Why couldn't this have happened yesterday when I was not working? What had she been thinking? How could this have possibly happened?

Afterward I asked Justine what happened. She was put in the basement jail cell with another woman or maybe a few women. She was absolutely devastated, as you can imagine. She cried for hours and hours. I asked her what they gave her to eat and if they provided her medication. Always the mother, I was worried sick about her and wondered if they were looking after my child. There had been an article in the newspaper very recently about the conditions of the holding cells. The article said that the prisoners were only given a processed cheese sandwich on white bread. Justine was a vegetarian and she would eat that but I wondered if that was what they gave her. I was also concerned about her medication. What she told me haunts me to this day. She said that although she was there thirty six hours they gave her nothing to eat, didn't provide any medication, and would not even give her a sanitary napkin even though she screamed and called for one. I was horrified! I know they don't want to make it comfortable for people who break the law but not even a pad? And nothing to eat? I was also concerned that missing two days of her medication would throw her back into depression or mania after we worked so hard to find one that seemed to work. I know what she did was unthinkable but to me that was inhumane.

The next day or so is not easily retrievable in my memory. I'm sure I have tried to block it out or I was in shock. I do remember booking off sick the second day of school and going to court. I had only been in a courtroom twice before and that was on a field trip for Grade twelve law and jury duty. I was both humiliated and ridden with shame to be there involved with my daughter's drug trafficking charge. Parents are treated with the same distain as the criminals themselves. After all, we raised them and looked after them! It must be our fault! It was an extremely humbling experience. We were made to wait hours and hours, sitting in a hallway with other criminals' families, and it was excruciating. Police and lawyers walking by and seemly looking down at the sorry lot of us. I wanted to explain that we weren't like the other parents. We were good parents! I really had to take an honest look at how I had judged other parents when their child had made a very bad decision. Sometimes people make bad choices despite good parenting.

When we finally were called into the courtroom after the entire morning of sitting, an hour lunch break, and most of the afternoon, I realized I could have gone to work and come afterward and not missed a thing. Everyone is expected to be there for nine o'clock in the morning. but the cases get called as the lawyers and judge are available and ready and this could be any time. At one point, the lawyer told us we would have to come back tomorrow. It was overwhelming to think that Justine would have to stay another night in jail. Luckily, we got a break, and they called us in around four o'clock.

I thought Justine would be there, but we could only see her on camera from the police station. She was in handcuffs and her hair was all matted. She was wearing the same clothes she had been in since the previous morning. She was crying uncontrollably and had huge black circles under her eyes. Because she had been off her medication. I could see a wildness in her eyes. The audio at her end must've been poor, and she was struggling to hear what the judge was saying. It was causing her distress and frustration. Without any sleep and no medication, I was holding my breath that she would not lose her temper. She was extremely on edge. I had been angry enough up to that point that I had not cried. The sight of her in this predicament traumatized me, and the floodgates opened up. I began sobbing. We held our breath as they held her fate in their hands.

They granted her bail and we had to go sign her out at the police station. They still had the paperwork to do so it seemed a very long time until she appeared. She practically fell into my arms from sheer exhaustion and surviving such an extreme ordeal. I thought she would never want to repeat that ever again.

We were named her sureties, which meant we were totally responsible for her until her hearing. If she messed up, we would lose our house. We certainly drilled that into her. She could go to work and school but no-where else without one of us with her. It was worse than when she was a teenager. At least then, we had allowed her to go out, even though we worried. I have no idea how long it was until her trial. It's all a blur.

I do remember going to another court where Greg, Justine, and I sat for hours as her lawyer ran around in and out of the courtroom bringing us tidbits of information. It was another all-day affair, breaking for lunch and going back and waiting again. One more day of missing work when I could have gone. That was the least of my worries, however. There was a chance she could serve jail time.

We were hoping for house arrest, and thankfully she got a year of house arrest. This meant a year of her wearing an ankle bracelet. She had to record each time she left the house and each time she returned. She was allowed to work and go to school. We were no longer responsible for her, but she lived with us, and she was home more than she had ever been since childhood. Surprisingly, it seemed easier knowing she was the police's responsibility and not ours. We didn't worry every time she left the house. We actually bonded again that year. There was no arguing or power struggles like when she was a rebellious teen. She knew she screwed up and was rather well behaved as I recall now. We spent a lot of time together talking and laughing. It seemed to be an easy year.

The day the ankle bracelet came off was the day I began worrying again. Suddenly, she was free again after a year of confinement. We knew she might go a little crazy, understandably. I was rather confident that she had learned her lesson however and we would not ever have to go through that ever again. I was right about the first part but wrong about the second part.

RIDING THE ROLLER COASTER

Justine had many ups and downs over the next year but the ups seemed to be more than the downs. The marketing program fit her lifestyle and she could continue working at the restaurant. She managed to get to most of her classes and get her assignments completed. Sometimes she got overwhelmed, but for the most part she was able to keep up with it all. We were really proud of her when she announced that she would graduate. We marked her convocation date on the calendar, but we nearly didn't make it to her graduation and neither did she. She should have known the police would be watching her. She was arrested again for drugs.

This time Justine went from the holding cell in the Oshawa Police Station to the Lindsay Jail. In one way, I was happy she was released from that terrible place where she got no food or even a pad, even though we were very angry with her and had to drive longer. Here she would be fed a real meal and hopefully would be treated with dignity, I reasoned. Again, it seemed we waited forever for the paperwork to be completed before she was released. When she finally appeared I asked her if it was a better experience.

"It's a jail, Mom!" she answered, meaning no! Again I had to take a deep breath and realize that I couldn't protect her. She kept getting herself into these messes and had to accept the consequences. The drive home was mostly silent. There was no point lecturing a grown woman who has made the same mistake twice. She knew she was in big trouble.

Greg went to court alone this time and I went to work. I couldn't keep taking days off to sit in a court hallway all day. I did know there was an even greater possibility she would be sent to jail, and in a small way, I hoped she would so she would learn a lesson. House arrest, however unpleasant, didn't seem to be doing that. It was time for "tough love."

When I asked her what the hell had she been thinking she responded that she needed the money to pay her lawyer's fees. We could have used our lawyer, but she didn't like him and for good reason. When she initially was charged, Greg told me that the lawyer talked to Greg about her, in front of her. She was an adult, and she felt very insulted. She chose to get her own lawyer and therefore had huge bills to pay. There was no way we were going to help pay for her mistakes. We were already risking our house each time we had to post bail. She was sinking into debt.

She graduated from her marketing program a few days later. I remember feeling so conflicted. Should I be proud or disgusted? How would she find a good job with a criminal record? Was all that schooling for nothing? I so wanted good things for her but she kept choosing bad things. What would her future hold? We made the best of it and took her out for dinner afterward. We told her we were proud of her accomplishment. It certainly wasn't easy holding down two jobs and going to college. Just like her disorder, she was doing good things as well as bad in equal measure.

Right at the start of something good, it looked bleak. She had gotten a marketing position with the company that did the setups for the hardware store she had worked at during high school and was juggling that job with her restaurant job. I feared she would lose it all. We spent another long day waiting in the hallway of a different courthouse. It was very touch and go with her lawyer zipping in and out of the courtroom and keeping us up to date. We weren't allowed to go into the courtroom for the sentencing this time and just sat in the hallway waiting. Her lawyer appeared before us with the news. One year of house arrest. I was a little shocked at that sentence. I thought, no wonder there are so many repeat offenders. I was very relieved too. House arrest made my life easier. She wasn't able to get into any trouble but could still work. Here we go again!

We spent another year together in relative ease. Our family was getting the hang of living together without the worry. In some ways I think Justine liked it too. She had no choice but to just toe the line. Her ankle bracelet was always in plain view. It was summer and she wore shorts and skirts. She always covered it for work. She and I even went for pedicures while she had her ankle bracelet on. The women at the shop would point and giggle. Justine would just laugh. I had to admit that I laughed too. It was what it was.

She travelled daily to different stores to do the set-ups and was always on the road. Justine had a really bad sense of direction. I tried many times to show her north, south, east and west on maps but she seemed to have a mental block and could not grasp the concept. She was an intelligent person, but she had difficulty finding her way around using directions.

One time when we were going somewhere and she was driving I told her to turn right and she turned left. That's an easy mistake and I'm sure we've all done that one time or another. I said,

"Just turn around at the next side street and we'll go back". She got very adamant and continued going the wrong way. She said,

"I can't do that! I have to go all the way around the block to where I started." I was aghast! What? I repeated that we should just turn around but she got angry with me so I sat silently as we drove all the way around a city block back to where she had made her mistake and we turned right.

One other time she had a job interview in a town north of the city. I told her what exit to take off the freeway and to go directly north and she would get to her interview on time. A half an hour later she called and said she hadn't seen the sign for the town on the freeway. I told her there would be no sign but that she was supposed to take the exit I had mentioned. She had driven right through the city and was driving out. I told her she'd have to turn around and go back. Needless to say, she was late for her interview.

I was constantly concerned that she had to find her way to different stores in different towns and cities. She bought herself one of the very first GPS systems ever made and this eased both of our worries. She still got lost sometimes but it was much better.

HOT TUB SURPRISE

When Justine was nineteen, Greg and I celebrated our twenty-fifth wedding anniversary. I wanted to take a trip to western Canada and recreate our honeymoon trip with visits to friends and family who lived in the western provinces. Greg wanted to have a garden party at our house. We decided to take a two week vacation out west and come home to get ready for one hundred people attending our beef barbecue in the following two weeks.

After our wonderful holiday, we arrived home to find a hot tub sitting in front of our garage in our driveway. Justine had been making payments on it for months and had asked a few relatives and friends to chip in for an anniversary gift. What a wonderful surprise! The only problem was that we needed it moved to our back deck and soon! Luckily, our wonderful neighbours, friends and relatives came to our rescue and spent many hours getting our deck ready, changing our wiring, installing a cement pad, carrying an extremely heavy tub around the house into the backyard and getting it hooked up and running all in time for the party.

As I write this chapter, that same hot tub is still used daily thirteen years later. Greg and I enjoy sitting, soaking and chatting when I get home from work and we use it all year in all weather. It sits three feet from the patio door of our bedroom so we can access it very easily. It is by far the best gift we have ever received from our generous and resourceful daughter.

HOME IS WHERE THE HEART IS

Justine lived with us until she was twenty-five. We always wanted her to be independent, but with her unstable moods, it was difficult for her to take the next step in her life and get a place of her own. That all changed when she was arrested for the third time. Greg and I threw up our hands and decided tough love was in order. Bailing her out for a third time was not going to solve anything. We always had a policy in our parenting philosophy that you got three strikes and then you're out. This was the final straw.

Leaving your child in jail is heart wrenching, even if you feel it is for his or her own good. I was devastated. Sometimes being a good parent is the hardest part. I just knew if we kept enabling her, it would continue. When she called from jail, she had already made a plan. She knew we weren't coming to her rescue this time.

She had called her good friend, Glenn and he had agreed to post bail for her. I was not in favour of this idea at all. I didn't want Glenn to put his house up and then be responsible for her. This was not going to teach her the lesson she needed to learn. I called Glenn and expressed my concern. I told him not to do it. Glenn was forty-five years old. He and Justine had met at the Hardware Store, when Justine worked in the paint department and he was a kitchen department manager one winter. He was a landscape architect and worked for a pool company every summer. He had a big three-story house that was in the middle of renovations but it was fully furnished with beautiful antique bedroom furniture.

He said "I know Justine doesn't have a criminal mind. I think I can help her turn things around." She moved in with Glenn and he became her surety for the year while she once again served house arrest and wore an ankle bracelet.

Glenn enjoyed having Justine live with him. He had lived alone for a few years but he really settled in with a roommate. They grocery shopped together and enjoyed making meals. Glenn set Justine up in grand style in a huge bedroom with a four-posted antique bed, dresser and a separate bedroom as her private dressing room. He even made her a huge rack for all her shoes. She parked her vehicle beside his house because her insurance had skyrocketed and he drove her everywhere. She was living like a queen.

That year was one of the best years for bonding as mother and daughter. Justine and I started walking together. It was a promise we made to each other to do on a regular basis. Most days I would meet her at her house after I finished work and we would grab a bottle of water and head over to the walking path. I often wish now that I had taken pictures because the trail is very beautiful at different times of the year.

In June, the peony gardens are in full bloom with hundreds of different varieties and brilliant coloured blooms. The horticultural society has an annual peony festival, but we avoided the crowd and meandered through there by ourselves. Justine, I'm sure, was not at all interested in looking at flowers with her mother but she did it for me. The spectacle was breathtaking whether you were interested in gardening or not. The trail wound through a treed park and came to a lovely stone bridge which crossed a creek. As we walked farther, we walked alongside the water and entered another shady park. On the hottest days, these settings were a cool welcome.

While we walked we talked about what we thought, how we felt, what our plans were and what some of our frustrations were. It was comforting to have a trusted friend to confide in. We offered each other advice and often just listened to each other. Some of my fondest memories are of those conversations while we walked.

Other times, Justine would come to our place. We would walk through the village right out to the dirt road, past the horse farm. Often we would walk through the little park to the pond. A wooden bridge crosses over a small creek, and a little trail scattered with a few memorial benches where we would stop and read the plaques bearing the names of the people who died and their families. After our walk, we would go back to our place where Glenn was visiting with Greg and we'd have dinner together. In the winter, Glenn and Justine would come every week for Sunday dinner. It was wonderful. She seemed happy.

When the year was over, Justine decided to get an apartment of her own. She found a cute basement apartment in a house with laundry facilities. It was like a doll house with low ceilings and everything seemed miniature. It had everything she needed and even had a fireplace in the living room. I got her some furniture at an auction sale and she settled in.

She and I went into business together that year and became associates with USANA Health Sciences so I saw her often. She still didn't have any car insurance so I drove her to work often. Glenn helped too. She lived right on the bus route, but rarely had to take a bus. She eventually got a lower insurance rate and gained true independence, or so I thought.

Justine suffered from posttraumatic stress disorder, as well as bipolar I never really knew exactly what Sam had done to her, but she told me once that he dragged her up the stairs when she didn't want to go with him. He had also warned her not to tell anyone or he would find her. I didn't realize it at the time, but she was scared living alone. She told me afterward that Glenn would spend every night there. It was no secret that they had developed a romantic relationship while she lived with him. I was a little uncomfortable with it at first because of their age difference, but Glenn was so thoughtful and kind and he really was her (and our) hero. She made a decision to move back in with him.

She rearranged the furniture and started making Glenn's place her own. They made a pact to finally finish the kitchen renovation and set up housekeeping. They fixed the roof and it seemed things were going well for a while. Glenn was not receptive of some of Justine's "friends" and wisely so. These were not her real friends, whom she had many of. I'm not sure who these people were because she certainly never mentioned them to me. Just like her bipolar disorder, she had good friends and bad friends. She and Glenn would argue over some of her choices. They broke up. Justine needed a new place to live.

We had always told our kids that once they moved out, they would not be moving home again. This doesn't mean I wouldn't help in an emergency, of course, but I didn't want my grown children moving in and out and not becoming independent adults. I saw this practice happening with many families and I just didn't want my kids to use our place as a flop house.

Justine wanted a house with a pool. She had always been a swimmer and started looking for an apartment in a house. She had started working the night shift and found a basement apartment with a family upstairs. The pool was in the backyard, which was just outside Justine's apartment. It all sounded wonderful, except for the kids. I told Justine it would be impossible for her to sleep during the day with the children swimming right outside her apartment. She hadn't thought of that. She kept looking, but most apartments with pools were out of her price range.

She decided she would get a roommate. She wanted someone living with her because of her PTSD and her fear of living alone, as well as to help with the rent. She didn't know anyone looking for a roommate so she put in a few ads. She moved into a house where she had the upstairs and the owner lived in the basement. It was a roomy three-bedroom bungalow with a pool. The first roommate was a no show and Justine was getting worried.

As everything happened in Justine's life, her despair was short lived. Her very good friend, Layce was having some challenges with her fiancé and took refuge with Justine one weekend. She never went back home. Justine got the best roommate ever. They got along famously, and because Layce worked days and Justine worked nights, they each had the place to themselves during the week and looked forward to spending weekends together. They settled into a perfect living arrangement and they lived together until Layce was on a vacation cruise and got a call that her roommate had been killed in a car accident. Layce wasn't able to get home for the funeral.

JUSTINE'S NINE LIVES

The traffic was particularly heavy on my drive to work that morning and I wondered why. I found my answer when the news came on the radio. They had closed the highway because of an accident, and everyone was being re-routed. I was nearly late for work. When I arrived, I mentioned why I was late. A few of us sat around the table discussing the fact that a woman ran into a transport truck, as the news had reported. Since it had happened several hours before at 4:10 a.m., I figured the woman was either drunk or had fallen asleep at the wheel.

My morning was going as usual and I was in my second period when my department head came in and asked me to step out of the gym class for a minute. This happens fairly frequently because it's usually something confidential or we don't want to disrupt the teacher. I was curious but not alarmed.

Instead of stopping just outside the door, he continued walking out of the gym area and down the hall. He was making idle chit chat with me as we walked toward the office. This is when I began to become a little uncomfortable. The principal was standing in front of his office and held his arm out for me to enter. No one wants to be called into the principal's office! I wondered what I had done wrong.

When I opened the door, two police officers were there. Then I saw Greg sitting at the table and immediately I knew it was about Justine. Greg stood up and came toward me, hugging me. He said what I already knew.

"It's Justine!"

I thought, "I knew that! What, this time?" He continued but I honestly don't know the words he used. You'd think something like that would be imbedded in your mind forever. The rest is a blur. Walking down the hall to get my coat and purse. Telling a few coworkers along the way when they came up to me, seeing my devastation. Greg wanted to go to his older brother and sister-in-law's house. We went there for a short while, and Greg called our families. Then we drove home and everyone arrived and the food and flowers began arriving.

The next few days were spent with family, friends and neighbours. My sister flew in from Vancouver, and she and my other sister stayed with us. My mother and step-father drove home from Florida. We planned the memorial service, spent an afternoon and evening seeing hundreds of people at the funeral home, and greeted guests in the evening. It's all very vivid and blurry all at the same time.

Many people said the service was the nicest they had ever been to. We played a few songs, a few of her friends chose to speak and we had a really wonderful officiant who had been a teacher at my school before he retired. I had supported a student in his final class. Everything went very well.

We found that the accident that had made me late that morning was Justine's accident. She had not been drunk, fallen asleep or driven into a transport truck. She had been driving home from her night shift. She was going a little fast, not wearing her seatbelt, and a transport truck (likely) clipped her front tire when he was changing lanes. I say "likely" because he isn't even sure, but the police think that's what happened. Justine always wore her seatbelt but for some reason, not that time. Her nine lives were up.

I believe everything happens for a reason, even if we don't understand. Justine lived the life she was meant to live for the time she was supposed to live it. I never question why. It was meant to happen the way it did. I never wonder if she would have married or had children. It's pointless to think about what might have been. Her life had meaning and purpose just the way it was. I never think her life was cut short or she was robbed of a full life. Her life was just that. Her whole twenty-nine years on this earth was hers. It was an interesting and fulfilled one. Justine's life. Justine's story.

JUSTINE'S GARDEN

I had a vision of a "secret garden" so I chose a central spot at the back of the yard and surrounded it with a circular ring of boxwood. The decorative, metal ivy gates were added after I took a night school welding class. For years it housed an old wheelbarrow filled with petunias. Something was never quite right about it but I could never pinpoint why.

When Justine died I decided to make a memorial garden. The little circular garden that sat so centrally among my many gardens finally had a purpose and I immediately could see in my mind how it should look. Glenn came over, and he and Justine's dad built a winding path leading to a wooden rocking chair at the back. We explained our vision, and soon people came over bearing gifts of plants and garden art. It became a real community effort.

Purple was Justine's favourite colour so we filled the garden with shades of purple and pink. I wanted a designer daylily and found the perfect one. Justine had three tattoos. One was her surname on her wrist. The other two were on her shoulders. One was a tiny pitchfork and the other was angel wings. Just like in the cartoons where the devil and the angel whisper in the person's ear, encouraging his or her to do bad things and good things. They suited her perfectly. The yellow and red lily in the garden is called 'Angel on My Shoulder".

EPILOGUE

We can let our personal problems define us or can choose to move forward and use them to make us strong.

Raising a child who had mental health issues was never easy. It was terrifying and frustrating, compounded by isolation. Unless you know other parents who are going through the same thing you have no one who understands. Parents stay silent because they don't want to expose their children to the stigma. I doubted myself for years. Only after Justine became an adult could I look back and know I had done the best I could for her.

Then there were the arrests. Devastation, depression, embarrassment, humiliation, and fear were just a few of my life's daily occurrences. I couldn't protect my child anymore. What would become of her? What would people think of me? My daughter was a convicted criminal.

Every day I forced myself to hold my head high. I had not done anything wrong. I had not kicked her out. I had searched for help. I had found what was available at the time, which wasn't much. I loved her. I accepted her. I tried to encourage her. I tried to be strong. I was honest with family and friends. I shared what was going on. I had nothing to hide. I had no shame.

I was proud of Justine. Despite everything she managed to hold down a full-time and a part-time job. She graduated from college. She had a support network of people who loved her and accepted her. She was taking medication after many years of shunning it. She had her share of problems but she was functioning well most of the time. Things were improving, although there would always be highs and lows. We would just ride the waves.

Suddenly, it was gone. It had all been for nothing. Wiped out. Twenty-nine years vanished. The baby I carried for nine months in my uterus. The infant I breast-fed for six months. The smiling cherub that melted our hearts. The sweet girl she became. The tormented teenage years. The healing years of her adulthood. Gone!

How does a mother recover from such a loss? Some mothers never do. I was determined to not become one of those mothers. What good would that do? I wanted to make Justine's life matter and share her story so other teens would not feel alone. I wanted other parents to realize they aren't the only ones going through this. To stop the secrecy and stigma attached to mental health. I didn't want to spend the rest of my life mourning. That just isn't me.

I was born under the zodiac sign of Cancer the mother. I need to help. It's my calling. If you ever want to upset me, then tell me I can't help. I've worked with kids who have special needs since I was a teenager. If you ever want to rattle me, then exclude one of my students. I'm still a mother. I'm a grandmother. This book is my baby too. Just as Justine will always be.

<u>Justine</u>
Justine was a gift
Unexpectedly she came
Smile like all the earth
Tenacity was her fame
Imprinted in our mind
Never to forget
Everything she left behind.
-Cathy Lynn Brooks
<u>Poem for Justine</u>
She lived twenty-nine years
It seems like a dream.
We lost her one morning,
Driving on her way home.
That's when fate intervened.
She was almost there,
Almost to her place,

But the highway was mean.
We know she's in heaven,
Although not in the clouds.
She's somewhere green.
It's tropical there,
With ocean and sand,
Where she would beam.
We try to be happy.
For her we live on,
To honour our angel, Justine.
-Cathy Lynn Brooks

ACKNOWLEDGMENTS

Writing a book can become all consuming during the writing, editing, cover designing and publishing. I have such a great support system and everyone willingly lent a hand and put up with my constant chatter about the progress of this book.

I'd like to thank my husband, Greg who has been supportive of this project from the beginning, and my daughter, Candice for allowing me to expose parts of her life and for her tech support. To my entire family, who've been my cheerleaders throughout, especially my mom who has encouraged me since I decided to write and my sister, Karleen who wrote the tagline.

I'd like to express my gratitude to my friend, Kate for giving me the idea for the cover and especially to Ashley Barron for nailing my vision and producing the beautiful book cover. Many thanks to Lynda and Elaine for offering sound advice as my beta readers.

Thanks to my friends who've been interested and enthusiastic while I told my story.

Final thanks to Justine for choosing me to be her mom and taking me on this roller coaster ride.

FOLLOW ME

Website
Cathylynnbrooks.com

Instagram
@cathybrooks11

Facebook
www.facebook.com/cathylynnbrooks

Twitter
www.twitter.com/cathy_brooks

Tumblr
www.tumblr.com/blog/cathyynnbrooks

Email
cathylynnbrooks@gmail.com

Made in the USA
Columbia, SC
22 March 2018